"I JUST HAPPENED TO GLIMPSE AND SEE **THIS THING** RUNNING ACROSS THE YARD, A GOOD-SIZE **MAN OR** SOMETHING— LOOKS LIKE A MAN, I DON'T KNOW WHAT IT WAS, IT JUST RAN ACROSS THE YARD."

"THERE IS NO REASON TO BELIEVE THEY ARE AGGRESSIVE IN ANY WAY . . . NO REASON TO BE AFRAID."

"THE CREATURE WAS NOT TRYING TO HURT ME IN ANY WAY. I BELIEVE IT WAS JUST CURIOUS ABOUT ME, WONDERING WHAT I WAS."

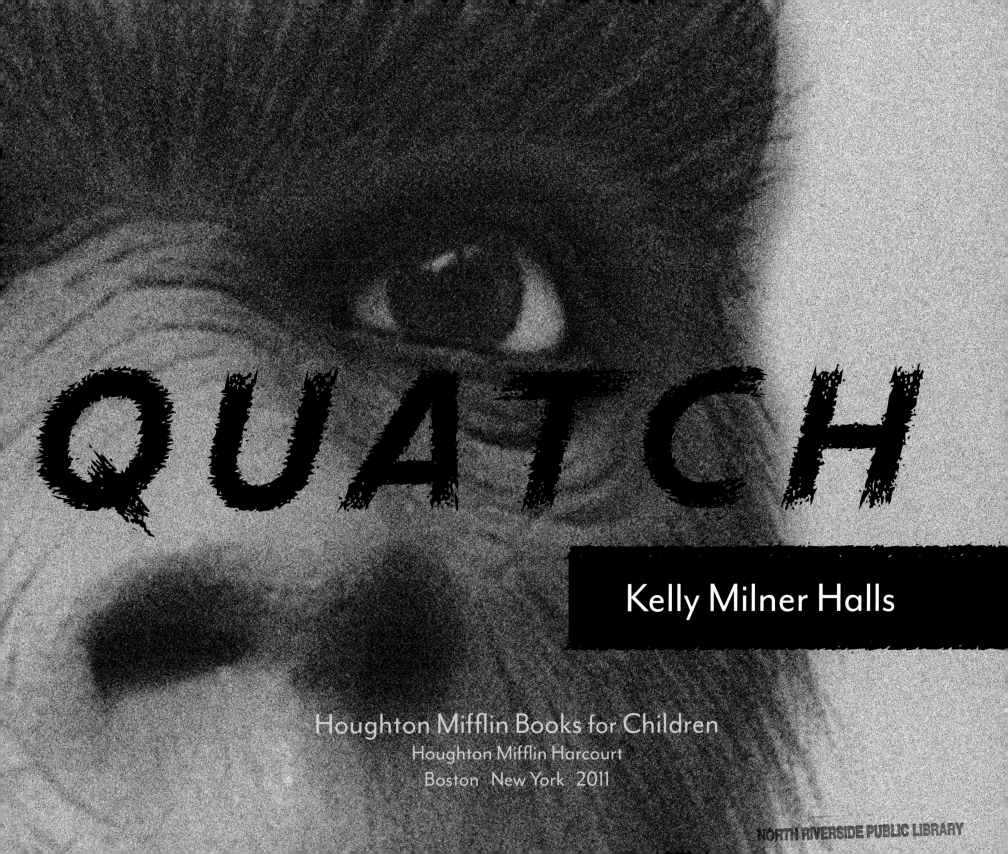

QUATCH

Kelly Milner Halls

Houghton Mifflin Books for Children

Houghton Mifflin Harcourt

Boston New York 2011

Houghton Mifflin Books for Children is an imprint of Houghton Mifflin Harcourt Publishing Company.

www.hmhbooks.com

The text of this book is set in Sentinel.
Photo and illustration credits appear on page 40.

Library of Congress Cataloging-in-Publication Data

Halls, Kelly Milner, 1957–
 In search of Sasquatch / Kelly Milner Halls.
   p. cm.
 ISBN 978-0-547-25761-7 (hardcover)
 1. Sasquatch—Juvenile literature. 2. Cryptozoology—Juvenile literature. I. Title.
 QL89.2.S2H35 2011
 001.944—dc22

                    2011005785

Manufactured in China
LEO 10 9 8 7 6 5 4 3 2 1
4500304085

SASQUATCH, ALSO KNOWN AS BIGFOOT, IS CONSIDERED A CRYPTID— A CREATURE OF CRYPTOZOOLOGY.

Acres of wilderness remain unexplored.

What is cryptozoology? According to author and cryptozoologist Loren Coleman, it is the study of creatures not formally recognized by traditional science. It is the quest to understand eyewitness observations that simply cannot be proven via ordinary channels.

Coined by French-born zoologist Dr. Bernard Heuvelmans in the 1960s, the term *cryptozoology* is based on the Greek word *kryptos,* which means "hidden." The word and its origins made Coleman smile. What a perfect definition, he said, for a sometimes imperfect set of scientific goals.

Why imperfect? Because "hidden" animals are hard to find, hard to believe in, and, if you're not the person who had the close encounter, hard to prove. Science depends on evidence—careful and repeated documentation. And not everyone believes a creature like Sasquatch is real.

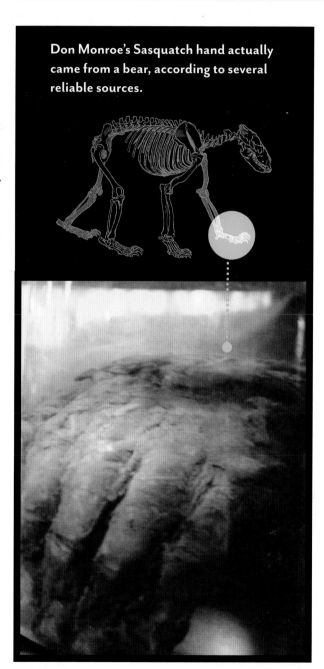

Don Monroe's Sasquatch hand actually came from a bear, according to several reliable sources.

Are experts such as Loren Coleman discouraged by this skepticism? Nope, not even a little. Serious Sasquatch hunters are as skeptical as unbelievers. They are not out to collect great stories. They are out to put together facts. Proof. The difference is, they are willing to keep an open mind.

Sasquatch and its cousins around the world have escaped capture so far, but other mysterious animals once considered cryptids (undocumented mystery animals)—such as the giant squid and coelacanth—have *eventually* been confirmed. So as long as cryptids leave trails of scattered clues, cryptozoologists will keep trying to put the puzzle pieces together, especially when it comes to Sasquatch.

Sasquatch experts like Coleman and anthropologist Dr. Jeffrey Meldrum, pictured here with the author, believe that the mystery behind Sasquatch will be solved.

THOUSANDS OF PEOPLE BELIEVE IN *IT.*

Hundreds say they have seen it. Many have found compelling bits of evidence as they've hiked dusty forest trails and snow-packed mountains to find it. But the truth is still uncertain. The mystery of Sasquatch has not yet been solved.

What might Sasquatch be? The answer to that question depends on who you ask.

The term *sasquatch* was identified in the late 1920s by the Canadian journalist Ralph Burns, based on the First Nation Indian tribe's Salish word for the hairy giant. Broader interest in the apelike biped, a creature that stands on two feet, began in 1957, when the Texas oil tycoon Tom Slick first funded the search for Asia's mysterious biped—called Yeti—in the mountains of Tibet.

A decade later the Patterson-Gimlin film, shot by Roger Patterson and Bob Gimlin in northern California in 1967, made Sasquatch a household name. But centuries before Burns, Slick, Patterson, or Gimlin made their claims, thousands of Native Americans had eyewitness accounts of their own.

Dozens of tribal legends mention an oversize "hairy man."

In the Beginning: Native American Tales

Described as everything from a spiritual "big brother" to a baby-stealing cannibal, Sasquatch was known by many different names among North America's indigenous peoples. But its physical description was almost always the same—seven to twelve feet tall, covered in brownish hair.

"He is seen as a special kind of being, because of his obvious close relationship with humans," wrote the Kootenai Indian author Gayle Highpine in the Western Bigfoot Society newsletter, the *Track Record,* in July 1992. "Some elders regard him as standing on the 'border' between animal-style consciousness and human-style consciousness, which gives him a special kind of power."

In the Kootenai tradition, Sasquatch is an animal of the natural world—a beast clever enough to escape capture, but no more mystical than any other animal. Modern Sasquatch hunters agree. In other tribal stories it is a creature of supernatural strength. In addition, "Among many Indians . . . the Hopi, the Sioux, the Iroquois and the Northern Athabascan, he is seen as a sort of spirit being whose appearance to humans is meant to convey some kind of message," Highpine wrote in the *Track Record.*

What kind of message? It could be a warning to resist human evils, she explained. Our move away from kindness and common sense may have upset the natural harmony of life on Earth. Sasquatch sightings may be a call to restore balance before it's too late.

The author-anthropologist Kathy Moskowitz Strain retold stories and compiled a list of more than 130 unique "hairy man" names from Indian folklore in her book, *Giants, Cannibals and Monsters: Bigfoot in Native Culture.* These stories are not always as kindhearted as Gayle Highpine's account.

Oo-wel'-lin, the Me-wuk Indians' "hairy giant," reportedly traveled the California countryside, eating people. The Yokut tribe's "Hairy Man" listened for the sound of women pounding acorn meal so he could steal it from their mortar bowls.

A Comanche medicine woman named Sanapia described a fur-covered cannibal, twelve feet tall, called Mu pitz. To keep him happy—and full—tribal elders set out food for him. When they found the bones of Mu pitz on the plains of Texas and Oklahoma, they ground them into a powder to treat bone injuries.

Colville Indians in Washington State saw their Skanicum, or "Stick Indian," as a clever shape-shifter, able to take the form of a tree to escape capture. Though he ate roots and other ordinary foods, he was known to kidnap humans for companionship, including a young bride in one story.

Did the regional creatures really have a taste for kids, or did native parents simply use the stories to scare their children into more cautious behavior? "It's hard to say," said Strain, "but it is still a part of their culture today. And tribes that believed Sasquatch to be helpful—even a creator—still practice the songs and dances designed to honor it, too."

A Yokut tribal basket featuring the woven image of Sasquatch.

A Yokut costume tribute to their ancient stories of "Hairy Man" or Sasquatch.

Why Did Kathy Moskowitz Strain Care?

As a child, Kathy saw the 1972 movie *The Legend of Boggy Creek,* and it put her on the path to her future. The fictional retelling of the Fouke monster—a three-toed, Sasquatch-like creature in Fouke, Arkansas—captured Strain's imagination and set her on the prowl.

"My teacher told me that in order to study Bigfoot, I would have to become an anthropologist, so that is what I did!" Strain said. "During the day I am the forest heritage resource and tribal relations programs manager in Sonora, California. At night I look for Sasquatch with my husband, Bob."

Though she has never seen the mysterious animal herself—so far—she has been spurred on by her husband's eyewitness experience and countless interviews she conducts with other people who have seen it themselves.

"As a scientist, my goal is to prove that Sasquatch is a real creature," she said. "I do this through several methods. First, through the nonprofit Alliance of Independent Bigfoot Researchers, I try to educate fellow researchers to use the highest scientific standards while in the field. I also help analyze evidence collected. Second, I conduct fieldwork with my husband in our research area."

Approximately two thousand sasquatches populate North America, according to Strain's research estimates—ten to fifteen in her home county of Tuolumne in California alone. But does Sasquatch matter?

"I think in today's society, with so much technology and pressure on our time, it's nice to think that there is still something left out there for us to discover," Strain said in an interview with the *Sacramento Bee* newspaper, "something still wild and free."

Reliable witnesses say that Sasquatch, also called Bigfoot because of the large tracks it

has allegedly left behind, is smart and curious but shy. It sometimes watches people from a safe distance but has no desire to interact with them. "There is no reason to believe they are aggressive in any way," says the Idaho State University anthropology professor and Sasquatch expert Dr. Jeffrey Meldrum. "No reason to be afraid."

Regardless of what the creature is called, the mystery remains. A growing number of serious scientific Bigfoot hunters believe it is really out there, and they are determined to prove it. They don't see the gentle giant as a monster. They see it as an unidentified North American great ape, a missing link between the known great apes—gorillas, orangutans, chimpanzees, and bonobos—and man.

How is the search for Sasquatch expanding now that serious scientists such as Dr. Meldrum are involved? Is Sasquatch real? The evidence might convince you that it could be.

The author and anthropologist Kathy Moskowitz Strain has studied Sasquatch extensively.

Sasquatch, Bigfoot, Yeti, Yowie, Yeren, Skunk Ape: these are all international names for what may be the same mysterious animal. But there are many other names less familiar. The author and anthropologist Kathy Moskowitz Strain has invested years gathering stories of Sasquatch from Native American eyewitnesses and other reliable sources. Here are just a few of the names she has documented.

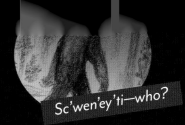

Sc'wen'ey'ti—who?

TRIBE	TRADITIONAL NAME	ENGLISH TRANSLATION
Cherokee	Kecleh-Kudleh	Hairy Savage
Chickasaw	Lofa	Smelly, hairy being that could speak
Chinook	Itohiul	Big Feet
Hoopa	Oh Mah	Boss of the Woods
Hopi	Chayeyu	Giant
Iroquois/Seneca	Ge no sqwa	Stone Giants
Navaho	Ye'iitsoh	Big Giant
Puyallup/Nisqually	Steta'l	Spirit Spear
Shoshone	Dzo'avits	Cannibal Giant
Sioux	Chiye-tanka	Big Man
Spokane	Sc'wen'ey'ti	Tall Burnt Hair
Tsimshian	Ba'oosh	Ape or Monkey
Wenatchee	Choanito	Night People
Yakama/Klickitat	Qui yihahs	The Brother (hairy)
Zuni	Atahsaia	Cannibal Demon

Stone Head Artifacts

Ancient artifacts—some carved up to seventeen hundred years ago—have been found in or near the Columbia River basin in Washington State and Oregon. Hand-etched stones, roughly the size of baseballs, reflect strange images, at least for a North American locale.

"Among the many stone carvings were a number of heads which so strongly resembled those of apes that a likeness at once presents itself," wrote the Yale explorer and dinosaur hunter Othniel C. Marsh in his 1877 expedition notes.

This discovery is important because, other than man, there are no records of advanced primates on this continent—no apes. And yet ancient people often carved their likenesses in stone and wood. Could those works of ancient art be tributes to Sasquatch? A growing group of serious scientists think so.

Most of the unusual relics are in museums and private collections all over the world now, but they pop up from time to time—sometimes in the strangest places. In 2008 the Sasquatch enthusiast Tony Pleschia found a rare carving—examined and currently being researched by Kathy Moskowitz Strain—for sale on eBay for fifty dollars.

Why were these artifacts carved in the first

Ancient artifacts found near Oregon's Columbia River resemble apes.

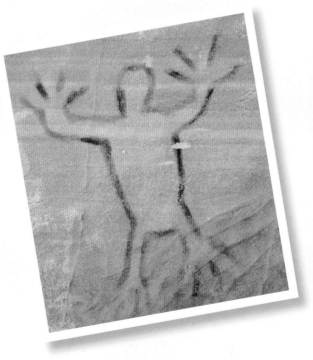

Mysterious rock art that could depict Sasquatch.

place? "Some archaeologists believe that when a native person creates a piece of art, it is meant as a 'prayer' to gain power over that animal," Strain said. "A hunter may paint a herd of deer as a way to have a great hunt. A shaman—or medicine man—may carve a stone head to control an animal in a certain way.

"We know that Sasquatch is represented in various art forms, including pictographs (rock paintings), totem poles, and basketry, as well as in songs and dances. But why each culture created the art—the reason for its creation—may never be fully known."

Native people shared their stories in stone.

TWO THINGS COME TO MIND WHEN POWERFUL EVIDENCE OF SASQUATCH IS MENTIONED— FOOTPRINTS OR TRACKS LEFT IN SAND, SOIL, OR SNOW; AND PICTURES OR FILMS.

With the discovery of convincing physical evidence came an increased determination to confirm it—including a scientific competition between the Americans and the Russians more than fifty years ago.

Tom Slick's Race with the Russians

According to the *Humboldt Standard* newspaper in Eureka, California, in January 1952 the National Geographic Society mounted an expedition to Tibet. They were in search of a rare, cannibalistic spider found only in the highest reaches of the Himalaya Mountains. But also on their observation list was what

The oil man Tom Slick searched for the Yeti in Tibet.

locals called a "giant, shaggy, manlike beast"—the Abominable Snowman, or Yeti.

A year earlier, the British explorer Eric Shipton had returned from a trek to Mount Everest with photographs of giant multitoed footprints. Intrigued by the images, the Texas oil millionaire Tom Slick decided to fund expeditions of his own in search of the Asian cousin to Sasquatch.

According to newspaper reports, Slick made it to Nepal in April 1957 and, after six weeks in the Barum Valley region, captured footprint photos of his own along with a clump of dark hair. The beast itself evaded him. Because he considered it a "vital missing link in the theory of evolution," Slick soon planned a second expedition.

"It could be a new type of anthropoid ape, a type more advanced than a gorilla," Slick said in the *Odessa American* newspaper in June 1957. "We talked to quite a few natives who said they saw the 'snowman' and a lot of them identified ape photographs as looking a lot like him."

Seven months later, in January 1958, a Russian expedition from Leningrad State University set out to capture the beast before the Americans could return. Professor Aleksander Pronin, who led the team, was reportedly the first non-native to actually see the Yeti himself. Now the quest became personal.

By February, Slick and a second expedition team were back in Tibet and the race was on. The goal, according to the expedition leader Gerald Russell, was to film the Yeti in its natural habitat, and they had until the end of May to make it happen. They returned in June without success, but they remained convinced that the creature was real. Russia also failed in their mission to capture the Yeti.

According to the *Lethbridge Herald,* a Can-

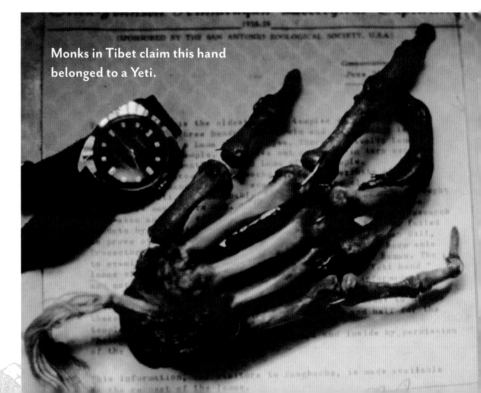

Monks in Tibet claim this hand belonged to a Yeti.

adian newspaper, a mummified Yeti baby was allegedly discovered and shipped to Moscow for study in 1959. But it was lost in transit, never to resurface again.

Slick's team, according to his friend and fellow expedition member Peter Byrne, secured the mummified finger of a Yeti hand from a Buddhist monastery in Tibet. Smuggled out of the country by the film actor Jimmy Stewart and his wife, Gloria—allegedly hidden in her underwear to avoid closer inspection—the finger made it to the British scientist William Osman-Hill, who confirmed that the digit was not human.

The author Loren Coleman got written confirmation from Stewart before he passed away, admitting that he and his wife helped Slick bring the artifact out of Tibet. But the finger was lost once Hill completed his analysis in London. Where could it be? "Probably among a wealthy private collector's prized possessions," Coleman said—another Sasquatch mystery to solve.

The Patterson-Gimlin Film

Roger Patterson, a rodeo cowboy, and his friend Bob Gimlin ushered in the next wave in Sasquatch mania, led once again by a series of tracks. Longtime believers, the two men were drawn by reports of lengthy paths of tracks

The actor Jimmy Stewart and his wife, Gloria, smuggled an alleged Yeti finger out of Europe while he was in the U.S. military service.

called "trackways," made up of footprints between fourteen and sixteen inches in length. Patterson rented a professional-quality movie camera, and they headed for Bluff Creek, California, in October 1967. On horseback, they rode into the rugged backcountry—miles from any human contact—hoping to find evidence of their own.

As he and Gimlin rounded a bend in the creek, Patterson captured a glimpse of something unfamiliar, even strange. His horse reared in alarm and fell in the soft sand of the riverbank—on top of his rider. A seasoned horseman, Patterson tried to calm his mount long enough to get out from under it and to pull the movie camera from his left saddlebag. Then he let the frightened horse go.

According to a radio interview, Patterson yelled to Gimlin, "Cover me!" as he ran toward the creature, roughly 120 feet away. Still on horseback, Gimlin dismounted and drew his rifle from the scabbard to train it on the animal.

Both men had agreed never to shoot a Sasquatch if they found one. They weren't prepared to kill the mysterious animal just to prove it actually lived. But Gimlin wouldn't let this creature attack his friend—not without defending him. His anxious finger rested on the trigger.

Images of "Patty" from the 1967 Patterson-Gimlin film represent compelling evidence of Sasquatch's existence.

Patterson knew he had the proof he needed, captured by the camera. So he ran, breathless and determined, after his goal, but he soon tripped on a raised sandbar and fell, which was all visible in the movie footage. Quickly Patterson righted himself and tried to refocus the camera.

Though much of it is a blur, Patterson captured one minute of film that autumn day—one minute and six seconds, to be exact. Today that footage, called the Patterson-Gimlin film, is considered the most convincing piece of visual evidence ever secured. Dozens of experts have studied it. Some have called it a hoax or a fake—a man in an elaborate ape costume. But most consider it authentic.

Hollywood costume and special effects expert, Bill Munns, agreed. After more years of careful study, Munns said, the muscular flexing visible in the film would be impossible to create even in an expensive, twenty-first-century ape costume. How could it have been accomplished more than forty years ago? He also said that the anatomical proportions of the creature are not right for a man in a monkey suit.

"The arms are too long," he said at a 2009 lecture, and a man's head would never fit in a mask shaped like the head in the film. "He could never see out of such a mask, even if you could make it fit," he continued. The creature also had visible feminine features—breasts—something never featured in ape costumes of that era, or today. That explains why experts often call the film's star Patty.

Even the hair of the Sasquatch in the Pat-

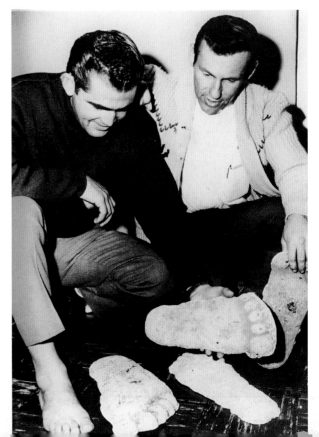

The rodeo cowboys Roger Patterson and Bob Gimlin captured powerful film evidence in October of 1967.

terson-Gimlin film—not fur, but hair—was impossible to create in movie costumes made more than forty years ago. "It's fluid," Munns said. "It moves just the way human hair moves." Costume fabric with that kind of authenticity had not been created in 1967.

"I believe," Munns concluded, "the film is almost certainly real."

The Patterson-Gimlin film remains the most famous footage of Sasquatch ever recorded. But it's not the only one. Several other short films look promising when it comes to Bigfoot authenticity.

Bill Munns, a Hollywood special effects expert, believes the Patterson-Gimlin film is not a hoax.

Hide-and-Seek Sasquatch

As a twelve-year-old, Montra Freitas had an experience in 1978 that most Sasquatch seekers would consider a dream come true. She came face-to-face with one of the world's most mysterious creatures on a shady path in a rural California campground, long before nightfall.

"I went with my parents to the Sugarpine Campgrounds," she said, "and I was bored out of my mind." With no one to play with, Freitas wandered down toward a gentle creek to play by the water. As she walked the distance, roughly one city block, through the thick pine forest, she got a strange sensation.

"I had the feeling someone was watching me," she said, "and the hair on the back of my neck stood up a bit." Not yet afraid, Frei-

Though Roger Patterson has passed away, Bob Gimlin stands by their story nearly fifty years later.

tas slowly turned clockwise, her eyes searching as she moved. Once she came full circle, she saw, from a distance of fifteen feet, what looked like an arm gently wrapped around a huge old-growth pine.

Freitas said, "I could make out long fingers and very dark brown hair covering the entire arm. I thought, 'That's not a branch and it's not a bear's paw, but it sure looks like an arm with a hand.'"

She had pondered the thought for only a moment when a face peeked out from the other side of the large tree. "It was a very flat face, very dark brown. I couldn't make out any features, except for the eyes," she said, "and they were looking right at me."

Because the figure was slightly bent, Freitas isn't sure how tall the Sasquatch was, though she wonders if it might have been a juvenile, like her; as curious about her as she eventually was about it . . . eventually, but not right away.

Fear bolted up her spine. She had never heard of Sasquatch, had never spoken to people searching for proof of its existence. She knew only that she was alone in the woods, a full city block from the safety of her campsite, looking at something completely unknown.

Without another thought, Freitas ran, fast and hard, straight to her parents' camper, without once looking back. "I didn't tell my mom or dad about it, since I thought they'd think I was crazy," she said. "Needless to say, I stayed in the trailer for the rest of our vacation."

Thirty years later, she sees things a little differently. "I was really scared," she said, "but the creature was not trying to hurt me in any way. I believe it was just curious about me, wondering what I was. If it had meant me harm, it could have easily reached out and grabbed me as I ran past it on the trail. Maybe it was afraid of me, too. I wish I hadn't been so scared. I wish I had kept my cool long enough to interact with it."

If she had, Montra Freitas would have made Sasquatch history. But she'll be ready the next time the opportunity comes around. And she's definitely hoping there will be a next time.

Making Tracks

When a Sasquatch footprint is found, investigators make every effort to document and preserve it. Whenever possible, photographs are taken before the track is disturbed. Often, a familiar element such as a ruler, a dollar, or a pencil is photographed beside the footprint to help mark the size and scale—to confirm how big the track really is.

Once photographs are taken, experts prepare a cast of the footprint. A cast is a molded copy of the footprint itself. It preserves every detail of the track, long after weather and time have erased the original impression.

Some experts use plaster of Paris—the same white powder mixed with water and used as cement in craft and construction projects. But when it dries, plaster of Paris is soft and fragile. So other experts have switched to dental plaster, the sturdy material dentists use to make molds of people's teeth. Law enforcement officers also use dental plaster, called dental

stone, to collect impressions as evidence at crime scenes.

Sticks and leaves resting gently on the surface of the footprint are carefully removed. Then the plaster is mixed and poured as a liquid into the track. Once the plaster dries, it is very carefully lifted out of the original track so it can be transported back to a research facility or office for further study.

Where the track cast was made is carefully recorded in case experts want to return to the location for future study or observation. If Sasquatch once walked down a forest path, it might pass that way again. Keeping careful records is important to science and exploration.

Plaster casts are used in many scientific fields to capture evidence. For step-by-step instructions on casting Sasquatch tracks of your own, see the Project Bigfoot website at projectbigfoot.brinkster.net and click on "How to."

When she was twelve, Montra Freitas came face-to-face with Sasquatch.

Montra still has dreams of Sasquatch.

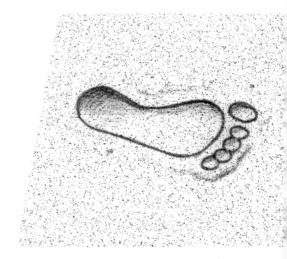

Sasquatch 911

In 1996 a man on the Kitsap Peninsula in Washington State called 911 to report an intruder outside of his house. Several sources report that the man saw a Sasquatch but was afraid the police wouldn't come if he mentioned the creature by name. So he said it *might* be a person.

The public information officer Scott E. Wilson at the Kitsap County Sheriff's Office confirmed the call as authentic. He also confirmed that the 911 operator is still employed by the county.

Read the transcript below, or listen to it on YouTube, but ask your parents first: there is some strong language featured on the actual tape. Did the Kitsap man see Sasquatch or a *very* big man wrapped in something black? Check out the call, and decide for yourself.

Operator: 911, what are you reporting?

Man: Well, we've got someone or something crawling around out here.

Operator: Did you see what it was? Was it a person or an animal?

Man: I can't tell. All I know is my sensor light came on and I just happened to glimpse and see this thing running across the yard, a good-size man or something—looks like a man, I don't know what it was, just it ran across the yard.

Operator: Okay. You've had problems in the neighborhood before?

Man: Yeah, my dog was killed here just recently. I don't know what it was. Whatever it is, I couldn't catch it if I was going to chase it, but whatever it was, it was standing up. I'm right here looking through the window, but I don't see anything. I don't want to go outside.

Pause

Man: Jesus Christ, you better—Theo . . .

Operator: Sir, hello?

Man: Get somebody *out here.*

Operator: What's going on now, sir?

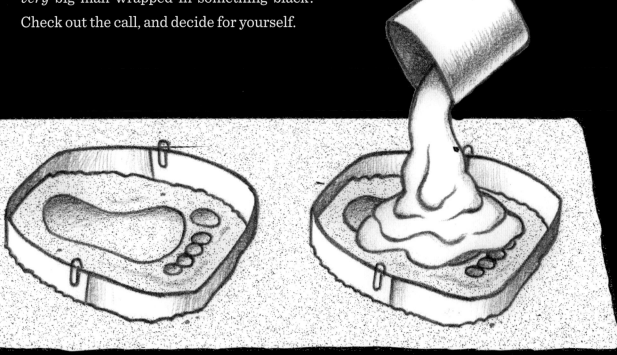

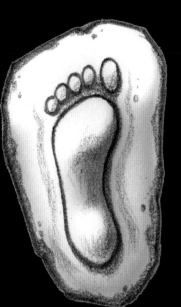

Man: That SOB is about six feet nine, I dunno...

Operator: Do you see him now, sir?

Man: Yes, I'm looking right *at* him.

Operator: Uh-oh. Okay, hang on.

Man: He's right...

Operator: Is he in your yard, sir?

Man: Yeah, and God, he's *big*.

Operator: What's he doing in your yard?

Man: He's lookin' at *me!*

Operator: And the guy is on foot...this...

Man: I don't know what, it's a *big*—it's a *real* big person, that's all I can say.

Operator: Okay, but it is a—it is a person?

Man: I, ah [*pause*], I—yeah, I'd say it was a person or somebody really big, but he's all in black.

Operator: Is it a black male or a white male? Do you actually see, or was he just wearing black?

Man: He's all black and he's big—he is *big!*

NEW TECHNOLOGIES

Language expert R. Scott Nelson believes Sasquatch families have their own language.

IF NEW EVIDENCE HAS BEGUN TO SURFACE IN THE SEARCH FOR SASQUATCH, IT MAY BE A DIRECT RESULT OF ADVANCES IN TECHNOLOGY. Science surges forward, and Sasquatch hunters are making good use of these evolving tools. So are dedicated scientists, from biologists to language specialists to outdoorsmen with a military approach. All are determined to collect evidence that might prove Sasquatch is more than a figment of any person's imagination.

Vocalization and Language

Like most fathers, retired U.S. Navy linguistics expert R. Scott Nelson helps his son whenever he can, especially when it comes to academics. But when Sasquatch became the topic of his twelve-year-old son Steven's proposed school report, Nelson had a skeptic's reaction.

"I am not and have never been a Bigfoot researcher," Nelson admitted. "Until recently, I have never had other than a passive interest in Sasquatch."

Even so, when Steven asked what sound a Sasquatch makes, Nelson did his best amateur imitation. "I let out a wailing moan," he said, "and Stevie responded, 'Dad, that's not what Bigfoot sounds like.'"

To settle the bet, father and son did an Internet search and discovered short samples of the Ron Morehead and Alan Berry tapes—Sasquatch vocalizations from California also known as the Sierra Sounds.

After twenty years as a cryptolinguist in the navy, Nelson was hard-wired to draw the truth from thin air—to recognize coded language in many international tongues; backwards or forward, fast or slow. Even today as the director of international programs at Wentworth College in Missouri, teaching Russian, Spanish, and Persian, Nelson deals with hard facts, not legends or wistful stories. But there was something about the sound files that made him sit up and take notice.

"I played it over and over and over," Nelson said. "I was intrigued. Finally Steven smacked me and said, 'Dad, what's the matter?' I told him what I recognized in these samplings—whatever these creatures were, they were using language. I knew it. There was simply no mistake about it."

Steven was doubtful. "Dad," he said, "how do you know it's a language? It sounds like apes fighting to me." Nelson explained that he'd have to do more research to be sure, and he set out to get original copies of those tapes.

"I sent out letters and e-mails to everyone I could find. Finally I got a call from a researcher who knew where I could find Ron Morehead. After I convinced him that I was not a crackpot, he said, 'You might be the guy we've been looking for—for thirty-five years.' The next day, the tapes were on their way to me."

After fifteen months of detailed study and consultations with his fellow linguistics experts, Nelson remained convinced. "I know it's language—because I have isolated too many elements of language within the vocalizations for it not to be language," he said. "There was more than one creature on the tapes—nonhuman creatures—and they were speaking in conversational terms of utterance, articulated individual units of meaning that were being repeated."

R. Scott Nelson (left) shares his research on Sasquatch language with dozens of believers in Yakima, Washington.

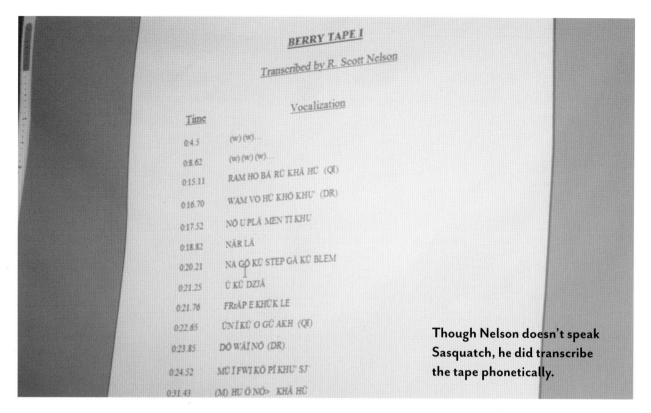

BERRY TAPE I

Transcribed by R. Scott Nelson

Time	Vocalization
0:4.5	(w) (w)...
0:8.62	(w) (w) (w)...
0:15.11	RAM HO BÁ RŬ KHÄ HŬ (QI)
0:16.70	WAM VO HŬ KHŌ KHŬ (DR)
0:17.52	NŌ U PLÄ MEN TI KHŬ
0:18.82	NÄR LÄ
0:20.21	NA GÓ KŬ STEP GÄ KŬ BLEM
0:21.25	Ŭ KŬ DZJÄ
0:21.76	FRĭÁP E KHŬK LE
0:22.65	ŬN Í KŬ O GŬ AKH (QI)
0:23.85	DÓ WÄI NÓ (DR)
0:24.52	MŬ I FWI KŌ PĪ KHŬ SJ
0:31.43	(M) HU Ō NÖ> KHÄ HŬ

Though Nelson doesn't speak Sasquatch, he did transcribe the tape phonetically.

Carefully stored in his pristine lab are more than one hundred footprint casts. Stacks of photographs have been documented, studied, and filed. Dr. Meldrum has even examined fresh footprints—the first, in 1997,

Dr. Jeffrey Meldrum of the University of Idaho believes Sasquatch may be real based on his study of the footprints they allegedly leave behind.

In a public statement released to mark the completion of his official research, Nelson said, "I believe that the study of these tapes will never and should never end. With the recognition and acceptance that these creatures do indeed speak and understand a complex language, a greater effort will be made to collect voice recordings, and our analysis of the language will improve.

"Now that we have a precedent and techniques established for this study," he concluded, "the process will certainly become easier."

Scientific Track Analysis

Dr. Jeffrey Meldrum is not a traditional "Bigfoot hunter." He is a highly respected professor in the Department of Biological Sciences at Idaho State University in Pocatello. And yet he is also on the Sasquatch trail. Why?

"Hundreds of large humanoid footprints have been discovered," Dr. Meldrum said. "Many have been photographed or preserved as plaster casts. As incredible as these reports may seem, the simple fact of the matter remains—the footprints exist and warrant evaluation."

outside of Walla Walla, Washington, on a muddy farm road. "They really sank the hook for me," he said.

First discovered by the longtime Sasquatch enthusiast Paul Freeman, the trackway featured thirty-five to forty-five clearly visible tracks, according to Dr. Meldrum. Each one was nearly fourteen inches long and more than five inches wide. Just before the rain gently washed his fragile evidence away, Freeman carefully captured seven of the footprints as plaster casts.

Analysis of these and other footprints was astonishing. Sasquatch, according to Dr. Meldrum, has what is called a flexible midtarsal joint, as do other great apes (bonobos, orangutans, gorillas, and chimps).

Both humans and apes have a midtarsal joint near the center of the foot.

Sasquatch track expert Bob Titmus cast this track in 1962.

But the human joint is rigid, locked in place to help form the arch—that gentle curve upward you can see on the bottom of your foot. Because apes have a flexible midtarsal joint, they have flat feet, with no arch. This flexible joint can even press downward when apes walk or run.

During the 1960s, the famed California taxidermist and tracker Bob Titmus made casts that displayed an obvious pressure ridge—the flex of the Sasquatch's midtarsal break. Careful comparison to earlier track casts revealed that the Titmus footprint was made by Patty—the female Sasquatch captured on the Patterson-Gimlin film in 1967. According to Dr. Meldrum, "Patty was responsible for a number of other Blue Creek Mountain tracks, just on top of the ridge above the Bluff Creek film site."

What is significant about Sasquatch having a flexible midtarsal joint? It means that the creature has an apelike foot rather than a human foot. And it matters because people trying to pull off hoaxes probably don't include that bend in the tracks they produce, and footprints that reflect the flexible midtarsal joint probably have not been faked.

Scientific study of Sasquatch footprints is one way experts are using technology to solve an ancient mystery.

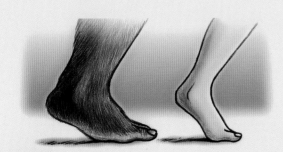

Sasquatch investigator Paul Graves captured this image of what may be a juvenile footprint belonging to a Sasquatch.

Motion Sensor Camera Mounts

Dressed in camouflage and full of confidence, Derek Randles looks like a cross between a military hero and the host of a television wilderness program. And it's a good thing, because his work as a Sasquatch investigator requires courage, strength, and stealth—another word for sneakiness.

Randles needs to be sneaky, because he heads up the Olympic Project—a focused attempt to capture Sasquatch photographs—in rural Washington State, where many sightings have been reported in the mountainous region. Carrying more than sixty pounds of complicated gear, he hikes into some rugged regions of the Pacific Northwest, above the ridgelines, where few humans ever go.

Dozens of Sasquatch tracks have been found at the ridgelines, along with the tracks of elusive predators, including bears and mountain lions. Randles wants to capture photographs of those camera-shy animals, using motion-triggered cameras called Reconyx RC60s.

Believing that the capacity to shoot at one frame per second and to store five thousand images on a 2.0GB CompactFlash card meant the potential for capturing powerful evidence, Randles was persuaded to mount up to five cameras in a single, promising location.

Other motion sensor cameras have been used to try to document sasquatches, without success. "I believe the animals may see the older camera flashes," Randles said, "and learn to avoid them." As the red flash of the camera trigger is engaged, more common animals, such as deer and raccoons, react. That recognition is often recorded in the very next photographic frame.

According to Randles, a smarter animal such as Sasquatch might learn that lesson from a safe distance. A more subtle camera had to be found, and the flash-free RC60 was the solution. The cost of the pricey cameras—roughly six hundred dollars each—came straight out of the investigator's pocket, but not all the problems were solved.

"Think of your living room," he said. "You can always tell when something is out of place, even if you've just walked into the room. For the Sasquatch," he continued, "the ridgeline is a living room."

Planted cameras, even quiet, non-flashing cameras, might be noticed by an intelligent primate such as Sasquatch. So Randles plans to camouflage the units visually. He and his partners are creating barklike faceplates to mask the unnatural look of the sophisticated equipment.

"I am confident," he said, "that with these cameras, we will eventually capture pictures of Sasquatch." He is so convinced that he's willing to make the grueling hike once a month to collect, replace, and reset the camera memory cards and batteries. He is also eager to do ongoing analysis of the images.

Derek Randles is one of the new technological wizards determined to find Sasquatch—in his case with an army of extra infrared eyes.

Sasquatch hunter Derek Randles has placed motion sensor cameras throughout Washington State's Olympic Peninsula.

Thousands of remote acres make the Olympic Peninsula the perfect habitat for Sasquatch.

Seeing Sasquatch—Sort of . . .

The artist and museum exhibit designer Rick C. Spears is best known for illustrating children's books and building fleshed-out dinosaur models. But when Georgia Bigfoot hunters asked him to create a bust (head and shoulders) of Sasquatch, he was more than up for the challenge.

What made you decide to create a Sasquatch sculpture?

I was asked by a guy who studies Sasquatch here in Georgia to make a life-size Bigfoot fig-ure to take to a Sasquatch conference in Tex-as. I started building it, but the conference was canceled that year, so I put the model on hold. I will finish it when I get the time!

What research did you do to prepare for this project?

I looked at a lot of pictures of the great apes to get ideas of different facial features, and I looked at what few Sasquatch photos there are. I also used knowledge I gained from working on other cryptid projects.

Is there any one famous Sasquatch that helped inform the look of your creation?

Yes! The world-famous Patterson-Gimlin Sasquatch! I tried to emulate the head shape and the "flattened" facial features.

How did you make his eyes look so real-istic?

I used Sasquatch eyes, of course! Okay, they are really glass taxidermy eyes. I used a hu-man-style eye, rather than animal-style, to

Rick C. Spears's sculpture "Grover"—named for Sasquatch scientist Dr. Grover Krantz —will be complete and on display in Texas by 2012.

give my model a bit more expression and a look of intelligence.

Why did you name him Grover?

I named him after the famous Sasquatch research scientist Dr. Grover Krantz.

Have you done any other Sasquatch projects?

I was fortunate enough to illustrate different types of sasquatches and other cryptid animals for the book *Tales of the Cryptids: Mysterious Creatures That May or May Not Exist.*

Are there sasquatches in Georgia?

Well, after some pranksters from Georgia made national news with their "frozen Bigfoot" hoax, people may not think so, but there have been sightings reported throughout the state of Sasquatch-like animals. A well-studied cast was recovered from the track of a Sasquatch near the Elkins River.

Spears poses with Grover, man to man?

and so we'll always have some exciting mysteries left in life!

Why have we yet to find a Bigfoot body, if it is real?

If something dies in the forest, it doesn't stay around for very long, because of scavenging animals. Dead things get chewed up, and their pieces are carried off. That's one thought as to why no body has been found—so far. Another, more interesting aspect is that perhaps the sasquatches bury the bodies of their departed.

Nature is the ultimate recycler.

Do you believe Bigfoot is real, and if so, why?

Yes, I believe Sasquatch is a real animal. There is a lot of evidence supporting such a creature—evidence that can't be explained away as something otherwise—and the study of this evidence is becoming more and more scientific every day. But do I hope we find out conclusively? Yes and no. I hope we someday find the remains of a Bigfoot that can be studied and proven to be an extant species of North American ape. However, I hope that no living Sasquatch is ever captured, so it can be free,

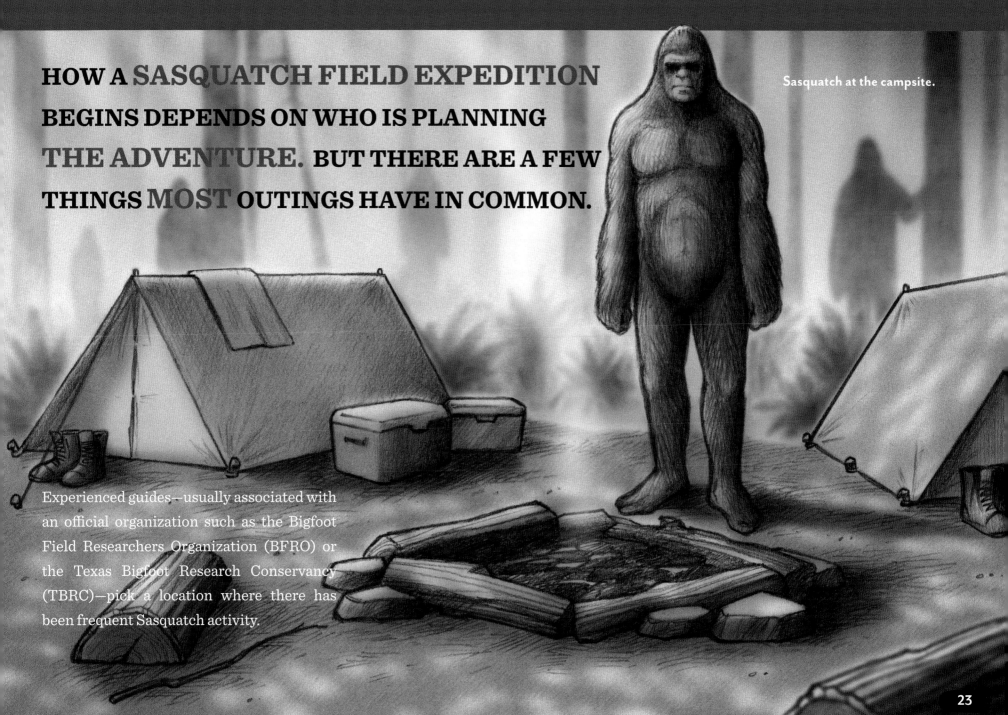

OUT IN THE FIELD

HOW A SASQUATCH FIELD EXPEDITION BEGINS DEPENDS ON WHO IS PLANNING THE ADVENTURE. BUT THERE ARE A FEW THINGS MOST OUTINGS HAVE IN COMMON.

Sasquatch at the campsite.

Experienced guides—usually associated with an official organization such as the Bigfoot Field Researchers Organization (BFRO) or the Texas Bigfoot Research Conservancy (TBRC)—pick a location where there has been frequent Sasquatch activity.

Where and When to Go

How do they know which places to pick? According to the Sasquatch hunter and musician Paul Graves, "There are certain areas that have a history of sightings. And once you've been doing this awhile you get a feel for the so-called hot spots—places that just have a Sasquatch feel to them. These creatures like swampy areas, and they seem to travel through ridgetops. There are many reports from high-altitude ridges."

Field researchers such as Cliff Barackman—who is a high school teacher in Oregon when he's not searching for Sasquatch—also help document "hot spots." They meet with eyewitnesses to record and document Bigfoot claims. They report on what the witnesses have seen and where they've seen it. If the stories are reliable, and if more than one report is filed from any given area, that place might be selected as a Sasquatch expedition location.

Once a promising spot has been chosen, a date is set for the adventure. Some people search for Sasquatch in the winter, and they are often successful. But remote locations can be tough to navigate in deep banks of snow. And some experts believe that Sasquatch activity jumps during the warmer months of the year. Thus, many expeditions are scheduled from May to September, when snow is less of a factor.

Once the location and date have been confirmed, teams are formed. Some are large—up to twenty people strong. Others are small, with only one or two people involved. Either way, each individual covers his or her own expenses—transportation, food, and other provisions.

Think of it as a camping trip, complete with hot- and cold-weather clothing, flashlights, tents, sleeping bags, cameras, film, toilet paper, and insect repellant—plus a little something extra. Sasquatch hunters—or

Sasquatch hunters hike for miles to remote locations like this one in Washington's Olympic Peninsula.

"Squatchers"—bring water and plaster for casting footprint tracks, hoping a Sasquatch will drop by to make them.

Keep Your Eyes Peeled

Tracks aren't the only signs of Sasquatch the expedition members might find by the light of day. Various trail markers are also considered Bigfoot evidence. "Some of them are called upbreaks," said Paul Graves. "Tree branches broken ten feet up, off the ground."

Could these breaks be natural damage due to bad weather? It's possible, but most Sasquatch experts note that the branches have been twisted, not simply snapped. They also note that these markers are the exception, not the rule. High winds did not snap all the branches in a single area, they say. Sasquatch twisted a single, solitary branch among many.

Along with upbreaks, there are small tepees—configurations of tree branches gathered from the ground and woven into structures. These are groups of roughly ten or fifteen sticks, far apart at the ground level, but gathered together to form a point at the top.

"We think they make them as some kind of marker," Graves said, "just as humans use road signs signs to find their way. They are woven so tight at the top, I can't pull them apart, even with substantial force."

According to investigators, Sasquatch has a grip far more powerful than the hand of a human being—a grip strong enough to snap a substantial branch.

Some Sasquatch experts believe these teepee-like structures may also be trail markers.

Investigators believe these broken branches called "upbreaks" may be Sasquatch trail markers.

Graves has also discovered what he considers a possible Sasquatch shelter. "I think it could be a den," he said, "and it's kind of volcano shaped. It's not a sure thing, but I'm not the only one to report them." The Duke University primatologist Carel van Schaik believes that orangutans build nests and shelters in their wilderness homes in Borneo and Sumatra, just as this Sasquatch might as North America's great ape.

Sasquatch itself might be sighted before nightfall, as was the case in the famous Patterson-Gimlin film, but in many cases the real fun begins after the campfires are blazing. As the forest grows dark, all eyes and ears are open and ready. Sasquatch could be just a heartbeat away.

Could this shelter be Sasquatch made? Paul Graves says it's one theory.

When the Sun Goes Down, the Beast Wakes Up

According to Cliff Barackman, "These creatures are largely nocturnal, very, very shy, and they do not expose themselves to human beings if they can help it." So actually seeing a Sasquatch, day or night, is unlikely. "They live like pilots who have been shot down behind enemy lines," he said, "and we are the enemy. They see how we treat other animals. They probably know what guns do. They don't want to have anything to do with us."

Though they seem to avoid being seen, they do not avoid watching people. Again and again, eyewitnesses report a sense of being watched in the darkness. They mention something from the dark beyond the campfire light tossing rocks or banging them together to make a sound. And it whistles and cries out, even when people are in close proximity.

Occasionally Sasquatch hunters capture a glimpse of what they call "eye shine." Unlike the reflective quality of a cat's eyes in the dark, when a flashlight hits the eyes of a Sasquatch, there is reportedly a soft glow of color as the light bounces off the moisture in the creature's eyes.

Moose Magnet, a member of Utah Squatching Group (USG), shared his report of a June 2009 incident on the USG website. The tracking experts Leigh Culver, Jason T. McAvoy, and Matt Pruitt had flown to Utah to teach local Sasquatch hunters how to track the creature more effectively.

As the weekend came to a close, Magnet and two other participants sat on a log, their backs to the tree line. "Within thirty seconds," he said, "a rock hit the log. We all heard it. I thought I had been seeing eye shine, but I didn't say anything."

Seconds later, a second rock flew from the darkness behind the three men and hit the log again. So Magnet confessed that he'd seen the reflective glow—a dull green. And the others confirmed that they'd seen it too.

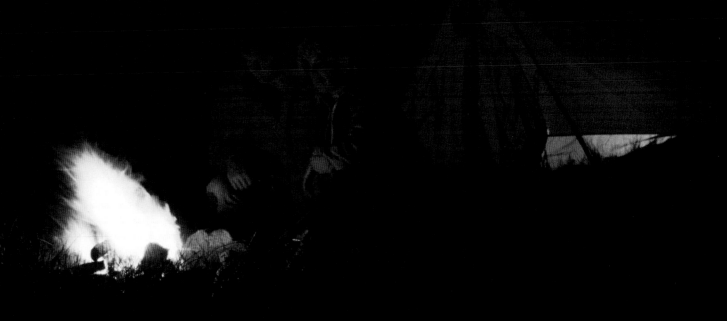

Teacher Schooled by Sasquatch

The Sasquatch investigator Cliff Barackman, a teacher, has been an enthusiast for more than thirty years. Drawn into the mystery by Dr. Grover Krantz, a Sasquatch expert and one of his professors at Washington State University, Barackman was transformed from a curious doubter to a true believer while he was in college.

Although he has never had a face-to-face encounter with a real Sasquatch, he does have a compelling field story, represented here in his own powerful words.

"My field partner and I were at a location in northern California a few years back in July. We went for a midnight walk with no lights and started making the noises we use to try to attract Bigfoot.

"We started hearing the peculiar 'chirp-whistles' and knocking sounds that have been associated with the animals, so we sat in the road and listened. Soon we heard two animals approach us from different directions. The animals were very, very quiet, but definitely coming in our direction.

"They approached us within forty or fifty feet, yet stayed off in the dense foliage. My partner then whispered, 'Are you hearing this one?' I said that I could hear them, and I pointed to the right, but to my surprise, my partner pointed off to the left and said, 'No, that one.'

"All at once, two things happened. The animal I pointed at to the right moved deeper in the woods (I guess Bigfoot doesn't like being pointed at), and the animal to the left made several brush popping noises as it stood up (I think it was crawling up to us). The animal on the left, now that its cover was blown, started stomping its feet and bellowing a grunt-huff-pouting noise.

"The noise was loud, gruff, and a little scary, even for two seasoned Bigfoot hunters. The huffy Bigfoot continued stomping the ground and huffing and puffing as it retreated down the hill into the ravine it had crawled out of. I never saw it, even though I scanned the area with night vision equipment. The next day, we found its path-way and tracked it into the ravine for perhaps a quarter mile. It was quite an adventure!"

Teacher and Sasquatch investigator Cliff Barackman, from Animal Planet's *Finding Bigfoot*, has studied the elusive animals for more than a decade.

Musical Camp Chairs

When Sasquatch hunters aren't scouring the dusty trails for supersize footprints or twig tepees, when they're not squinting to discover "eye shine" or dodging Bigfoot pebbles, they are gathered around the campfire, telling stories. If they're lucky, some of those stories are set to music.

Tom Yamarone and Paul Graves are happy to fill that distinctive niche.

Music was second nature for Yamarone, who grew up in California—one of the entertainment capitals of the world. Graves calls Washington State home, but his mother sang in musical theater. Both men wound up in the same creative zone, writing and performing songs about Sasquatch at conferences and campfires nationwide.

Why Sasquatch? "My first introduction was the Abominable Snowman on the *Rudolph the Red-Nosed Reindeer* animated feature," Graves said. But he's been pursuing serious Sasquatch leads for more than twenty years.

For Yamarone, it was living in the heart of Sasquatch country. "I was lucky enough to camp with my family in some amazing forests and mountains throughout northern California," he said. "At the Humboldt Redwoods State Park, where we camped every year, we would pass a gift shop called the Legend of Bigfoot." That, he said, is where it all started.

Today, both troubadours man acoustic guitars and entertain crowds of Sasquatch enthusiasts at every opportunity, thoughtfully writing their own songs. "I have written ten Bigfoot songs," Yamarone said, "and they've all come to me in different ways. But I don't try to write one every day. In fact, I'm happy to write one or two new songs a year."

"I have seven songs written," Graves added, "and I've performed five of them live. Sometimes a song will come to me in ten or fifteen minutes. Other times they evolve over a period of time. I wrote 'Bigfoot and Butterflies' in about fifteen to twenty minutes—words and music."

There is not a lot of money in Sasquatch songs, but cash isn't the point. "It's just a blast to play the songs," Graves said, "to see people's faces light up. I never get bored with playing Sasquatch songs."

"Some of the songs tell historic Sasquatch stories," Yamarone said. "Those are called ballads—songs that make the stories come back to life. Other Bigfoot songs are written to make you laugh and have a little fun. But I always try to be respectful of the subject, even when I'm writing humorous lyrics, because I

Sasquatch hunters, including Paul Graves, often set their adventures to music.

know many people have dedicated their lives to this search."

Are Graves and Yamarone Sasquatch believers?

"There is enough evidence in several areas to convince me they exist," Yamarone said. "Native American masks and carvings, pioneer newspaper stories, the Patterson-Gimlin film, hair samples, and eyewitness accounts—yes, sasquatches exist. Bigfoots are real. It's just a matter of gathering enough evidence to convince the general public."

Graves couldn't agree more. "I've talked to hundreds of people who have seen Sasquatch. These people come from all walks of life—the forest service, law enforcement, insurance agents, engineers, doctors, and hunters. They all describe the same creature and have for hundreds of years. It just doesn't make sense to assume it's a great big international hoax. Yes, I believe Sasquatch is real."

Tom Yamarone rocks his Sasquatch songs at conferences and in the field.

THE END—OR JUST THE BEGINNING?

UP UNTIL NOW, **YOU'VE EXPLORED** EXAMPLES OF EVIDENCE SUGGESTING THAT **SASQUATCH MIGHT BE REAL**, EVEN IF MANY CREDIBLE EXPERTS SAY IT IS NOT. **WHY?** THE ANSWER IS SIMPLE.

Dozens of other books and articles have proclaimed Sasquatch a hoax—an elaborate scheme to convince people that something unreal is actually real. And it's true that some Bigfoot hoaxes have been pulled off, nation- wide, including this recent example.

In the summer of 2008, a Georgia police officer named Matthew Whitton and his friend Ricky Dyer, a former prison guard, claimed they'd found the body of a Sasquatch in the mountains north of Atlanta. To preserve it, they said, they tucked it into an electric freezer, filled it with water, and literally put the lifeless creature on ice.

The Internet was on fire with speculation. The radio personality Tom Biscardi rushed to the scene and declared the find authentic. He even wrote a big fat check—some say a $50,000 check—to claim the corpse as his own.

Was Biscardi correct? No. He was not, as his associate Steve Kulls, executive director of Squatch detective.com, soon discovered.

As the ice began to thaw around the alleged Sasquatch body, Kulls "observed the foot, which looked unnatural, reached in and confirmed it was a rubber foot." Later that day, he said in a newspaper article, "both

Matthew Whitton and Ricky Dyer admitted it was a costume." It was a high-quality, expensive costume created by Chuck Jarman and available for sale at the Horror Dome—just $449.99 and it's all yours. But it certainly was not real.

Hoaxes do happen. And when they do, newspapers and television reporters all over the world make people aware of the dishonest schemes. That is a good thing. It protects us from tricksters and lies. But journalists don't always document more credible proof.

Have other cryptids like Sasquatch ever been confirmed? Yes, they have. For centuries, paleontologists—scientists who study extinct, fossilized plants and animals—believed the coelacanth was a 400-million-year-old prehistoric fish that vanished more than 65 million years ago along with the dinosaurs. Credible evidence "proved" that the coelacanth was no more than a fossil and had been for millions of years.

Truth shifted in 1938, when the museum curator Marjorie Courtenay Latimer went to the docks to examine a strange fish netted in the Indian Ocean off the coast of East London, South Africa. It was a coelacanth: a living fossil. It was a cryptid

Hoaxsters in Atlanta, Georgia used this upscale costume created by the Horror Dome (www.thehorrordome.com) to try to fool the public.

crossing from the land of myth to scientific certainty.

Coelacanth is not alone in the realm of cryptids proven real. The giant squid was once considered a legend. The Greek teacher and philosopher Aristotle told stories of the massive predator in the fourth century B.C. And in horrifying stories they could never quite prove, ancient seaman called it the Kraken.

Those courageous swashbucklers were vindicated in 2004. Motion sensor cameras financed and monitored by the National Science Museum of Japan and the Ogasawara Whale Watching Association finally captured a series of 556 underwater images of an

For centuries, Coelacanth was considered an extinct, prehistoric fish.

authentic giant squid off the coast of Japan. Legend became fact with the simple wink of a camera lens. Sound familiar?

Serious Sasquatch hunters believe their quest will one day be just as successful. And millions of people around the world are sure they're right. Until then, we'll have to be content with compelling evidence that has opened even skeptical scientific eyes to the possibilities. Do you believe? Consider the evidence; then see if you can decide.

In 2004, scientists photographed the fabled giant squid, which are an average of thirty-three feet long as in this illustration, but can grow up to a whopping fifty-nine feet long.

How big is your footprint compared to a quarter?

SASQUATCH SIGHTINGS IN NORTH AMERICA

According to experts at the Bigfoot Field Researchers Organization (BFRO), credible witnesses have reported seeing Sasquatch in every state in the United States of America except Hawaii, as well as most Canadian provinces. Their trained experts analyze each reported sighting and only document those that seem authentic or real. Is your neighborhood a Sasquatch habitat? Do some research of your own. The discoveries you make might amaze you!

LEARN MORE ABOUT IT

Books

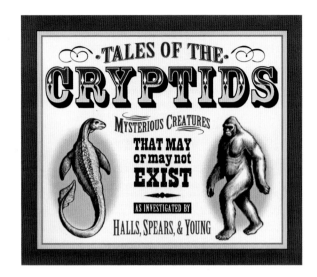

*Tales of the Cryptids: Mysterious Creatures
That May or May Not Exist*
By Kelly Milner Halls, Roxyanne Young,
and Rick Spears
Darby Creek Publishing/Lerner, 2006

Enoch: A Bigfoot Story
By Autumn Williams
Self-Published

*Cryptozoology A to Z: The Encyclopedia of
Loch Monsters, Sasquatch, Chupacabras,
and Other Authentic Mysteries of Nature*
By Loren Coleman
Fireside, 1999

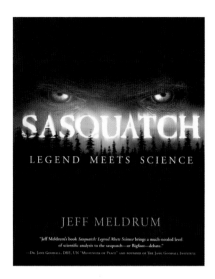

Sasquatch: Legend Meets Science
By Dr. Jeffrey Meldrum
Forge Books, 2007

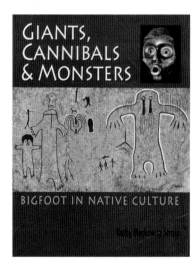

*Giants, Cannibals and Monsters: Bigfoot in
Native Culture*
By Kathy Moskowitz Strain
Hancock House, 2008

Bigfoot! The True Story of Apes in America
By Loren Coleman
Paraview Pocketbooks, 2003

Meet the Sasquatch
By Christopher L. Murphy
Hancock House, 2004

Videos

Sasquatch Science: Searching for Bigfoot
UFO TV, 2006

Sasquatch Odyssey: The Hunt for Bigfoot
Big Hairy Deal Films, Inc., 2004
CAUTION: Some adult language.
www.sasquatchodyssey.com

Monster Quest
Seasons 1, 2, and 3
A&E Home Video

The Legend of Boggy Creek
(Fictionalized)
Cheezy Flicks Entertainment
CAUTION: Some violence and adult language.

Websites

Bigfoot Field Research Organization
www.bfro.net

The Alliance of Independent Bigfoot
Researchers
www.bigfootresearch.com

Bigfoot Times
www.bigfoottimes.net

Cryptomundo
www.cryptomundo.com

Bigfoot Encounters
www.bigfootencounters.com

Oregon Bigfoot.com
www.oregonbigfoot.com

Texas Bigfoot Research Conservancy
www.texasbigfoot.org

The Bigfoot Museum
www.bigfootmuseum.com

Kentucky Bigfoot
www.kentuckybigfoot.com

The Bigfoot Recordings
www.bigfootsounds.com

Bigfoot Information Project
www.bigfootproject.org

Georgia Bigfoot
www.georgiabigfoot.com

Virginia Bigfoot Research Organization
virginiabigfootresearch.org

Michigan Bigfoot Information Center
www.michiganbigfoot.org

Eastern Ohio Bigfoot Information Center
www.eobic.net

Gulf Coast Bigfoot Research Organization
www.gcbro.com

Alabama Bigfoot Research
www.alabamabigfoot.com

Bigfoot Songs of Tom Yamarone
www.bigfootsongs.com

Photo and Illustration Credits

Page(s)

BIBLIOGRAPHY/SOURCE NOTES

Interviews by the Author

Cliff Barackman (teacher and Bigfoot investigator), May 16, 2009, June 26, 2009, July 8, 2009, July 13, 2009, July 29, 2009, August 7, 2009.

Dr. John Bindernagle (wildlife biologist), 2009, January 26, 2010.

Kirk and Cole Casey (outdoorsmen and track finders), May 18, 19, and 20, 2009, May 25 and 26, 2009, May 30, 2009, June 14 and 15, 2009, January 23, 2010.

Loren Coleman (curator of the International Cryptozoology Museum in Portland, Maine), May 11, 2008, June 13, 2008, July 29, 2009.

Paul Graves (Bigfoot investigator and musician), March 28, 2009, April 7, 2009, April 30, 2009, May 17, 2009, June 22, 2009, July 29, 2009.

Dr. Jeffrey Meldrum (Idaho State University), November 6 and 7, 2008, April 9, 2009, May 16 and 17, 2009.

Bill Munns (Hollywood special effects expert), May 17, 2009.

R. Scott Nelson (cryptolinguist), May 16 and 17, 2009, June 22, 2009.

Derek Randles (Bigfoot investigator), May 16, 2009.

Rick C. Spears (Bigfoot sculptor and illustrator), July 29, 2009.

Kathy Moskowitz Strain (anthropologist), July 8 and 9, 2009.

Deputy Sheriff Scott E. Wilson (Kitsap County Sheriff's Office), August 5, 2009.

Tom Yamarone (Bigfoot investigator and musician), March 27, 2009, April 3, 2009, April 26, 2009, May 16, 2009, May 22, 2009, July 5, 2009.

Articles

Bigfoot Field Researchers Organization article archive
www.bfro.net/GDB/newart.asp

Highpine, Gayle. "Attitudes Toward Bigfoot in Many North American Cultures." *Track Record,* July 18, 1992.

Vike, Brian. "Moricetown Bigfoot Tracks Continue Sighting Outbreak. British Columbia, Canada." *Interior News,* March 30, 2009.

Webster, Jack. Interview with Roger Patterson and Bob Gimlin. Vancouver, Canada: November 1967.
www.bigfootencounters.com/interviews/radiopatterson.htm

Books

Coleman, Loren. *Tom Slick and the Search for the Yeti.* Boston and London: Faber and Faber, 1989.

Cooke, Catherine Nixon. *Tom Slick Mystery Hunter.* Bracey, Va: ParaView, 2005.

Krantz, Grover. *Bigfoot Sasquatch Evidence.* Blaine, Wash.: Hancock House, 1999.

Meldrum, Jeff. *Sasquatch: Legend Meets Science.* New York: Forge, 2006.

Morgan, Robert W. *Bigfoot Observers Field Manual.* Enumclaw, Wash.: Pine Winds Press, 2008.

Murphy, Christopher L. *Meet the Sasquatch.* Blaine, Wash.: Hancock House, 2004.

Strain, Kathy Moskowitz. *Giants, Cannibals and Monsters: Bigfoot in Native Culture.* Blaine, Wash.: Hancock House, 2008.

GLOSSARY

anthropoid: a higher primate and/or human resembling an ape.

anthropologist: a scientist who studies human beings and their ancestors.

articulate: to form or fit pieces into a whole.

bonobo: one of a rare and very social group of apes similar to chimpanzees.

cannibal: one that eats flesh of its own kind.

cryptozoology: the study of mysterious or unknown animal species.

grueling: difficult to the point of exhaustion.

hoax: a trick meant to make people believe in something purposefully false.

humanoid: having human characteristics.

mortar: a sturdy bowl in which things are crushed or pounded by a second tool.

sensor: a device that responds to physical

stimulus such as heat, movement, sound, or light.

troubadour: a singer of folk songs.

tycoon: a businessperson of exceptional power and wealth.

INDEX

Page numbers in italics refer to illustrations.

"IT'S NICE TO THINK THERE IS **STILL** SOMETHING OUT THERE FOR US TO DISCOVER."

"IT JUST DOESN'T MAKE SENSE TO ASSUME IT'S A GREAT BIG INTERNATIONAL HOAX. YES, I BELIEVE SASQUATCH IS REAL."

"BIGFOOTS ARE REAL. IT'S JUST A MATTER OF GATHERING ENOUGH EVIDENCE TO CONVINCE THE GENERAL PUBLIC."

To Alex, Ava, and Anya —G. D.

To Sarah and Elmo —S. L.

LITTLE SIMON
An imprint of Simon & Schuster Children's Publishing Division
1230 Avenue of the Americas, New York, New York 10020
First Little Simon hardcover edition January 2016
Text copyright © 2016 by Greg Danylyshyn
Illustrations copyright © 2016 by Simon & Schuster, Inc.
For information about special discounts for bulk purchases, please contact Simon & Schuster Special Sales at 1-866-506-1949 or
business@simonandschuster.com. The Simon & Schuster Speakers Bureau can bring authors to your live event.
For more information or to book an event contact the Simon & Schuster Speakers Bureau at
1-866-248-3049 or visit our website at www.simonspeakers.com.
Designed by Laura Roode
The illustrations for this book were rendered digitally.
The text of this book was set in Comic SCF.
Manufactured in China 1015 SCP
2 4 6 8 10 9 7 5 3 1
Library of Congress Cataloging-in-Publication Data
Danylyshyn, Greg.
A crash of rhinos / by Greg Danylyshyn ; Illustrated by Stephan Lomp.
pages cm
Summary: Introduces in rhyming text the collective names used for various animal groups.
[1. Stories in rhyme. 2. Animals—Nomenclature—Fiction. 3. English language—Collective nouns—Fiction.] I. Lomp, Stephan, illustrator.
II. Title.
PZ8.3.D239Cr 2016
(E)—dc23
2014036792
ISBN 978-1-4814-3150-7
ISBN 978-1-4814-3151-4 (eBook)